# I, ISRAEL, ASK

A Spiritual Response to Love and Death

## In Combustion

Israel, is not what Israel
thinks Israel is...
...because Israel
in Oneness,
doesn't exist
other than
the verb Man

---

Full poem on page 122

Copyright © 2007 by Narda Azaria Dalgleish

Cover, typography and design by Narda Azaria Dalgleish
Printed in Great Britain by T J International

ISBN-13
978-0-9553759-0-3

OR'AZ PUBLICATION
oraz.pub@gmail.com
narda.lit@gmail.com
www.orazpublication.com
Responses are welcome

To my son Rotem Moria
may his mystery be elevated
in praise of He in whom all is re-collected

They gave me a glass of water
what do you see, they demanded
do you see it half empty
or half full?

Overflowing
I said, overflowing,
or else how could we,
the fingers, see we are all one
unless blinded in the Eye of the hand

# Contents

Introduction; Here is Love . . . . . . . . . . . . 9
The Taste of our Era . . . . . . . . . . . . . . . . 11
Acknowledgement . . . . . . . . . . . . . . . . . 15
Oh Ahmad . . . . . . . . . . . . . . . . . . . . . . 18
Oh Ahmad (Hebrew ). . . . . . . . . . . . . . . . 19
Welcome . . . . . . . . . . . . . . . . . . . . . . . 20
Oh Finger . . . . . . . . . . . . . . . . . . . . . . . 21
It is so Easy . . . . . . . . . . . . . . . . . . . . . 22
Between Como and Milan . . . . . . . . . . . 23
Abraham . . . . . . . . . . . . . . . . . . . . . . . 24
When Dead Before Death . . . . . . . . . . . 25
Sabbath . . . . . . . . . . . . . . . . . . . . . . . . 26
Love for Certain . . . . . . . . . . . . . . . . . . 27
I Never Cease . . . . . . . . . . . . . . . . . . . . 28
As You Are . . . . . . . . . . . . . . . . . . . . . . 29
Who is Elect? . . . . . . . . . . . . . . . . . . . . 30
Why? . . . . . . . . . . . . . . . . . . . . . . . . . . 31
Hear Love's Hover . . . . . . . . . . . . . . . . 32
If . . . . . . . . . . . . . . . . . . . . . . . . . . . . . 33
The Magnitude of Love . . . . . . . . . . . . . 34
Day of Din . . . . . . . . . . . . . . . . . . . . . . 35
The Breath of Kedem . . . . . . . . . . . . . . 36
Today . . . . . . . . . . . . . . . . . . . . . . . . . 37
Who Love Sees . . . . . . . . . . . . . . . . . . 38
Demand Now . . . . . . . . . . . . . . . . . . . . 39
Breathe Compassion . . . . . . . . . . . . . . 40
Certainty Waste . . . . . . . . . . . . . . . . . . 41
Damascus Market . . . . . . . . . . . . . . . . 42
Walk Away . . . . . . . . . . . . . . . . . . . . . . 43
My Mother's Tongue . . . . . . . . . . . . . . . 44
The Earth Answered . . . . . . . . . . . . . . . 45
Against me for me . . . . . . . . . . . . . . . . 46
Be Neither . . . . . . . . . . . . . . . . . . . . . . 47
I Wonder . . . . . . . . . . . . . . . . . . . . . . . 48
Come, Sit with me? . . . . . . . . . . . . . . . 49
You are not my Lord . . . . . . . . . . . . . . . 50
I Give Up . . . . . . . . . . . . . . . . . . . . . . . 51
Shocking . . . . . . . . . . . . . . . . . . . . . . . 52
ll: Da Capo, ad Infinitum :ll . . . . . . . . . . 53
Mercy, Mercy Speak . . . . . . . . . . . . . . . 54
Get Message from this Era . . . . . . . . . . 55
I am a Missile . . . . . . . . . . . . . . . . . . . . 56
Empty Suitcase . . . . . . . . . . . . . . . . . . 57
Perhaps . . . . . . . . . . . . . . . . . . . . . . . . 58
At Zero Greenwich . . . . . . . . . . . . . . . . 59
I, Israel, Ask . . . . . . . . . . . . . . . . . . . . . 60
January is a Dog . . . . . . . . . . . . . . . . . 61
Gladden my Face . . . . . . . . . . . . . . . . . 62
Nothing and No-one . . . . . . . . . . . . . . . 63
I Do! . . . . . . . . . . . . . . . . . . . . . . . . . . 64
Kisses upon Kisses . . . . . . . . . . . . . . . 65
Love is Didactic . . . . . . . . . . . . . . . . . . 66
A Sad Fashion Designer . . . . . . . . . . . . 67
A Concrete Noun in Hell . . . . . . . . . . . . 68
How Strange . . . . . . . . . . . . . . . . . . . . 69
The United Nations . . . . . . . . . . . . . . . . 70
…and before that… . . . . . . . . . . . . . . . 71
In the Middle . . . . . . . . . . . . . . . . . . . . 72
My Starting Point . . . . . . . . . . . . . . . . . 73
A Paramoral Poet . . . . . . . . . . . . . . . . . 74
Dare We? . . . . . . . . . . . . . . . . . . . . . . . 75
Jump in Dirty . . . . . . . . . . . . . . . . . . . . 76
Verb the Cow into Union . . . . . . . . . . . . 77
Lord of Dictionaries . . . . . . . . . . . . . . . 78
In Combustion . . . . . . . . . . . . . . . . . . . 79
How are You? . . . . . . . . . . . . . . . . . . . 80
Drown in Pleasure . . . . . . . . . . . . . . . . 81
Sitting in the Singular . . . . . . . . . . . . . . 82
My Soul . . . . . . . . . . . . . . . . . . . . . . . . 83
Have I Imagined? . . . . . . . . . . . . . . . . . 84
What is the Taste of Union? . . . . . . . . . 85
Copy Rights . . . . . . . . . . . . . . . . . . . . . 86
Woe to a Lover . . . . . . . . . . . . . . . . . . . 87
…So Corollarate . . . . . . . . . . . . . . . . . . 88
Detachment Woke me . . . . . . . . . . . . . 89
They Laughed . . . . . . . . . . . . . . . . . . . 90
One Lip . . . . . . . . . . . . . . . . . . . . . . . . 91
What is Said is Seen . . . . . . . . . . . . . . 92
To Palestine from Israel . . . . . . . . . . . . 93
What Say You? . . . . . . . . . . . . . . . . . . 94
A Word with You . . . . . . . . . . . . . . . . . 95
Covering up the Apparent . . . . . . . . . . 96
Charged with Itself . . . . . . . . . . . . . . . . 97
From which Essence . . . . . . . . . . . . . . 98
Give me to that Taste . . . . . . . . . . . . . . 99
An Adam Spat . . . . . . . . . . . . . . . . . . . 100
Ha Ha! She'd Better! . . . . . . . . . . . . . . 101
To Nogah . . . . . . . . . . . . . . . . . . . . . . . 102
Unquenchable . . . . . . . . . . . . . . . . . . . 103
In the Hum Hu . . . . . . . . . . . . . . . . . . . 104
The Grounds of Being . . . . . . . . . . . . . 105
Look who's Speaking . . . . . . . . . . . . . . 106
Jerusalem . . . . . . . . . . . . . . . . . . . . . . 107
Where Love Loves Love . . . . . . . . . . . . 108
An 'I' Inside Out . . . . . . . . . . . . . . . . . . 109
The hhhhh of He . . . . . . . . . . . . . . . . . 110
Your Hands Love . . . . . . . . . . . . . . . . . 111
In the 'I' of 'We' . . . . . . . . . . . . . . . . . . 112
I am not a Racist . . . . . . . . . . . . . . . . . 113
Blind . . . . . . . . . . . . . . . . . . . . . . . . . . 114
NeitherNor . . . . . . . . . . . . . . . . . . . . . . 115
How I-am-I Do . . . . . . . . . . . . . . . . . . . 116
Face to Face . . . . . . . . . . . . . . . . . . . . 117
Between All and None . . . . . . . . . . . . . 118
Patience . . . . . . . . . . . . . . . . . . . . . . . 119
Oh Lovechest . . . . . . . . . . . . . . . . . . . 120
When? . . . . . . . . . . . . . . . . . . . . . . . . 121
Translate an Eve into Eye . . . . . . . . . . . 122
Amidst Her Spires . . . . . . . . . . . . . . . . 123
Re-collection . . . . . . . . . . . . . . . . . . . . 124
Your Site of Encounter . . . . . . . . . . . . . 125
Lovethunderbolt . . . . . . . . . . . . . . . . . . 126
Interpreter of Twilights . . . . . . . . . . . . . 127
Her Musks at Dusk . . . . . . . . . . . . . . . 128
Talking to Love . . . . . . . . . . . . . . . . . . 129
Towards Encompassing . . . . . . . . . . . . 131

# INTRODUCTION

## Here is Love

In early October 1987, only a few months after moving from Tel-Aviv to a flat in Jerusalem, I moved yet again, not knowing that this would be the end of my residence in Israel. I flew to attend a six month course held in the breathtakingly beautiful landscape of the Scottish Borders surrounding the Beshara School of Intensive Esoteric Education. The new friends I met earlier in Jerusalem intrigued me. I bombarded them with questions and they reassured me... no, no dogmas, no gurus, no teachers... it is all between you and the One who is you...

During my first courses, more questions appeared... what does the One, or Oneness, mean to me?... to my essence?... does it make a difference to me whether the One names Himself He, She, It, the Absolute Unity of Existence, Beauty, Love, Compassion, or, God, as named in the religions?... how can I recognize my essence so that I know what it wants more than anything else?... who and what am I to the One?... can I be what I am to the One according to what the One is to His own Self?... how would it be like to know my being in union... permanently?...

One day, years later, my chest was filled with joy, and then, while still open and expanded it was seized, suddenly and without a seeming reason, by a worry unshakable for weeks... ...was it this that woke me up at nights to sit in lengthy contemplations?... ...what is essential Good News?... ...what a great mercy must it be for a heart to reach the firm certainty that its perfect aptitude for union overrides any habitual impediments, at any time and under any circumstance... ...is there a greater glad tidings for a heart than to be elevated to the point of vision of Oneness itself perceiving itself as the sole Being, Existence, Spirit, Consciousness and Matter of everything?... ...what might be worse, more sad or fearful for a heart than to be cut off or be distanced from the vision that only the One Lives, and hence, is Himself the Life and Light of all that lives and dies?... ...is my heart ready to give up the illusion of its self-subsistence?... is it ready to be of service to the perspective of Oneness?... ...to its love to be expressed originally?...

Were these questions to prepare me for what was to come?...

Exactly seventeen years after starting my first course, in early October 2004, still contemplating my heart in light of the great possibility given to mankind, I was struck by a formidable state of certainty... a presence of Love speaking - engulfing me immediately as I was told that my son, Rotem Moria, was blown up by Al-Qaeda.

Here, certainty has nothing to do with striving. Here, certainty allows grief; it is present even whilst one is far from being ready, understanding, pure or perfect. Here, certainty is brought about by Love, Love's own unveiling. In stark contrast to the situation, here is Love, unequivocally real in all faith, devotion, hope and belief, misguided though they may be. Here is Love, single indivisible Identity of all, including that of a son, his murderer and their mothers. Here is Love, irrefragable in the midst of terror. Here is Love, universal and personal. Here is Love, a centripetal movement seeking me in, while simultaneously 'shooting' me out like a missile, fuelled by and homed into Love's own impact.

Had it not been like that, the following responses would have remained private to me without even considering their publication. Quite possibly, they might not have arisen. As they did, my single intention was to refrain from habitual *dislocation* - however many years of studying the premise of unity, one stands before this instant as bereft of knowledge as one is before the first breath. No prior mystical state, taste, vision, knowledge or wisdom has any power whatsoever to either penetrate into the presence of this instant or to reanimate itself. How strange that we say 'knowledge is power' when cerebral increase, taken as means and aim, is dislocation from the very Presence of Love we seek. Here, Love alone is the conduit for its cognitive aim.

> Here, Love deems the
> lowest common denominator non existent
> while itself the highest collective factor

In the end, Love knows best its purpose. Where it is not met, one loves to be shown afresh, and where it is met, to Love belongs all praise.

## The Taste of our Era

Our era has opened up its chest in a massive outpouring. The most treasured mysteries hitherto held and guarded in the interior of mankind are now set before us as if in an exquisitely magnificent banquet, a feast of superb scents and tastes. This era pronounces directly and for the first time its timeless vision of unity in the collective 'we' globally; from the popular dictums such as 'we are all one', 'to reach our fullest potential', 'to know/be who and what we really are' etc., to the extraordinarily unprecedented international declaration 'We the Peoples of the United Nations... united for a better world'.

However conditioned or erroneous these pronouncements of unity may be, they nevertheless could not possibly occur unless absolute unity is our reality; unless intrinsically we are already unanimously obliged by our reality's perspective; unless we have the potential, aptitude and will to rise up to it perfectly, and unless it is our era's time to pioneer its unfoldment explicitly.

Our fullest potential
is a concrete subtle place wherein
when we become hidden, the Real is apparent.
Our fullest potential *is* the Real, the Beloved,
reachable immediately

In our era's taste, to know that we are *nonexistent apart from the One Being*, is the single most important prerequisite for understanding anything whatsoever, let alone our unity. Our collective we, has never been an accretion of beings. *We have never been* - individually or collectively. Nothing has ever been, is ever going to be or become by or in itself. The One Being is the becoming and the utter existence of our infinite diversity. How could we possibly know or be perfectly and completely who and what we are if we determine ourselves first, as separate autonomous existents and then qualify ourselves further by preposterous partiality?

Without this frame of reference, perfection is as unnatural - or rather supranatural - as Love is! Who could just like that, emulate the One who loves His own Self appearing as the Existence? However sophisticated, merely by our natural propensity we are imperfect, incomplete and denigrated even below the lowest natural form. Spiritual abjection however is eminence. The height of oneness is so by its incomparable infinite encompassing wherein the entire degrees of existence, from the absolute to the relative right down to the lowest of the low are included by an essential equality of identity.

The person brought to abasement in oneness is brought to its height of encompassing where he is shown clearly that the One is his existence as well as the existence of all, and that consequently, his existence was never his. This person may be called by his exterior form a human being, but by his reality he is a representation of the singular plurality, mankind. This reality is our universal DNA which qualifies us by its total identity and nothing less! To exclusively affirm or deny even a single phenomenon from existence, is to deny one's magnitude, to deny one's very being.

### Union is our essential education
### intimate to Love's manner of being

Only oneness is proof for oneness, and hence is itself the perfect aptitude in the 'who', the 'what' and the 'how' of our being. Our humanity starts solely and unequivocally from this high order of descent wherein the act of oneness is union and unification; it is a quid pro quo - one's totality for the One's totality, or one's illusioned identity for the One's reality.

Effectively union is re-cognition that oneness is not only actor but necessarily acted upon in all actions. Hence oneness aspires and is aspired to, in all our qualities, attributes and perceptibility. Long before we know of it and whether we admit it or not, the pull, response and preparation towards union are already the acts of union in union!

This newly emerging auto-didactic mode in our era, eclipses former secondary mediations by the unitive act itself without denying any. In the eye of union, all 'things' are necessarily reconsidered and expanded beyond their limited 'known-ness' into the unlimited munificence of the Known-to-itself, wherein they receive their most honourable due. This expansion of vision is ultimate freedom of choice, without which the most sincere student of oneness remains unsatisfiable and torn apart as he observes how the looped chain of endless apparent causes and effects respectively usurp an exclusive aggrandisement while condemning the rest to profanity.

The one touched by reality in the depth of his origin, even if he were to gather the weight of the universe itself as the total causality of human pains and suffering and then add it to his own, it would be stripped away at once and disappear irrevocably into non existence. In the absence of their causes, all pains and suffering are tasted as an incomparably intense attraction, Love's attraction towards its supreme happiness; therein, it is as if the bare universe is redressed with its original identity - Beauty in a perpetual love affair with Herself; Beauty is Lover and Beloved in all that loves and is loved, and the sole subject/object of all that loves and is loved.

Beauty's love affair
moves all towards Her view point

In vision, history itself is redeemed from its long and lonely exile in the captivity of the dim lights of the causality of diversity. From the first effusion of the most ancient origin into its universal consciousness manifested as relative time/space, nothing has ever happened other than the concatenations of the perfectible potential of Man. Our history spans, pans-out and expands from the timeless potential of all potentials to its most superlative completion of all completions; a globally unified humanity. It remains for our intrinsic unanimity to meet its greatest cataclysmic unfoldment yet, in the origin, here on earth, when the eyes and that which is seen are rendered naked.

# ACKNOWLEDGEMENT

It was a nice surprise to find out that a publisher, by the ISBN definition, 'is generally the person or body who takes the financial risk in making a product available'. Somehow it seems befitting that a book concerning the unity of humanity should have the very people who will read it offering its capital, thus indicating the real publisher. Deep gratitude to all the contributors, many of whom 'total strangers' who have donated and deposited in advance towards this book merely on the basis of reading 'Oh Ahmad', demanding no deadline or profit; to all the so many people for commenting, proof reading and encouraging; to my family Graham and Hannah for being so expansively accommodating, supportive and helpful.

How could I thank enough my friend David Apthorp whose wonderful creative agility complements a liberal spirit. He would ruthlessly chop off some material but more often persuade me enthusiastically to 'keep it!, yeah, yeah, yeah, keep it! keep it!', even when 'it' deviates from standard English. He would take a word or a sentence and delight in so many more inferences not shown at the time of writing. I am also profoundly indebted to Andrew Burniston, a stranger who appeared out of the blue, in the nick of time. To my astonishment he sat with me day after day offering invaluable comments which in the absence of a formal editor was a God send. Thanks to him I have expanded the introduction after he had very gently suggested that as it is, it may come across like a story of someone who reports that he had been abducted by aliens...

There is an old expression in Hebrew I have wondered about for years as it seemed too profound to be used casually. Literally it is 'I am imprisoned in gratitude', implying an immutable and permanent state of thanks. I say this now to acknowledge the Beshara School and its people, without whose example this book could not have come about. This example may be best illustrated in Joseph's reply to Pharaoh, who, when asked to interpret his dreams, said: 'Without me, God will answer...'

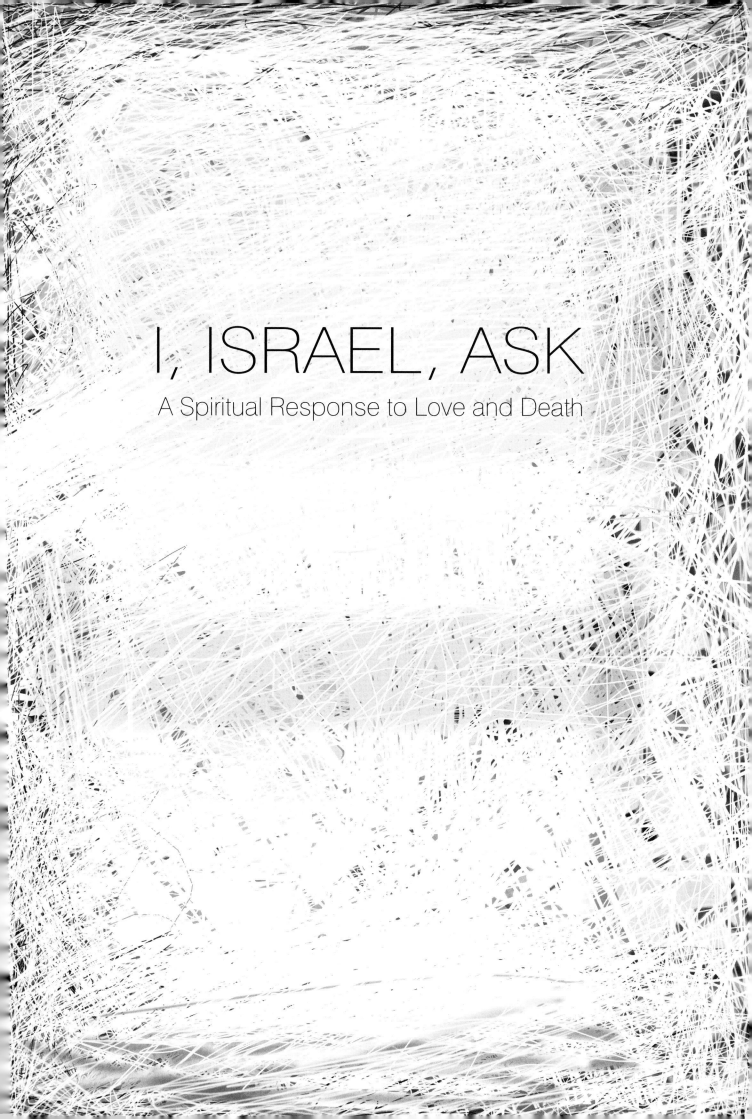

# I, ISRAEL, ASK
## A Spiritual Response to Love and Death

2002 and 17 October 2004

## Oh Ahmad

There is nothing I can do or say
to prevent your intention
to blow yourself up
with those you hate.
But I would like you to know anyway
that at the end of your last prayer
when you turn your head to the
right
and say
*asalâmu 'alâykum wa râhmat u-llah wa-barakâtuhu*
you have greeted me too
as I am there, right beside you
with the whole of Mankind
because your Lord is my breath

Then, when you turn
your head to the
left
and repeat for the last time
*asalâmu 'alâykum wa râhmat u-llah wa-barakâtuhu*
I am there too, with the whole universe
because everywhere you turn
there is His face
and your Lord is my breath

Even when
your hands and forehead touch the ground
and you say to your Lord with a deep sense of fulfilment
*Hu*
we are all there
right beneath you
with our foreheads and hands and knees and toes
touching yours from the ground.
So, just before you press the button
with your call *Akbar*
know that we are always between you and your Lord
because
He is our breath

---

*asalâmu...* - Peace be upon you (plural) and God's Mercy and Blessings.
*Hu* - He, the Absolute Ipseity, in Arabic, Hebrew and Aramaic.
*Akbar* - A Divine Name, the superlatively Greater.

This poem was initially conceived in 2002 in response to 9/11. As it is addressed to the essential being of a suicide bomber the name 'Ahmad' was chosen for its reference to the Divine Name the superlatively Praised.

## הו אחמד

אין דבר ביכולתי לעשות או לאמר
כדי למנוע את כוונתך
לפוצץ עצמך
עם שׂנואי נפשך.
אך בכל זאת הייתי רוצה שתדע
שבסוף תפילתך האחרונה
כאשר אתה מסובב ראשך
לימין
ואומר
"אַסַאלַמוּ עַלַיְיכּוּם וַוּרַאחְמַתוּלִלַה וַוּבַּרַכַּאתוּהוּ"
ברכת אותי גם כן
שהריני שם, לידך,
עם האנושות כולה
כי ריבונך הוא נשמת אפי


אחר כך, כאשר אתה
מפנה ראשך
שׂמאלה
וחוזר בפעם האחרונה
"אַסַאלַמוּ עַלַיְיכּוּם וַוּרַאחְמַתוּלִלַה וַוּבַּרַכַּאתוּהוּ"
הריני גם שם, עם כל העולם
מפני שלכל אשר תפנה
שם פניו
וריבונך הוא נשמת אפי


אפילו כאשר
ידיך ומצחך נוגעים בארץ
ואתה אומר לריבונך בתחושה של הנשמה עמוקה
"הוא"
כולנו שם
מתחתיך
כשמצחינו וידינו וברכינו ובהונותינו
נוגעים בשלך מתוך הקרקע.
אז רק לפני שאתה לוחץ על הכפתור
עם קריאתך "אַקְבַּר"
דע שאנו תמיד בינך לבין ריבונך
היות
והוא נשמת אפינו

25 October 2004

## Welcome

Welcome pain
welcome in my chest
even if you seize it
relentlessly tight

Stay as long as you will
but were you to speak
let me not forget
it is not his voice
nor is it my lament
but it is You, Love, it is You

25 October 2004

## Oh Finger

why are you all by yourself
while we are palmed single handed?

where could you be beside the Palm
who in itself was never outside Adam?

Oh Palm in the midst of We and we
is it not so whether or not we agree?

so which is your legacy
Oh finger, which will it be?

when we are concurred with; Adam is Adam
and when Adam is both We and we,

to where on earth d'you think
you're gonna flee?

26 October 2004

## It is so Easy

it is so easy for me to transcend You from any fault or limit
and protect You in praise when You hide in sheer beauty

but when manifest and of Your appearances
some are highly unpleasant, it is not at all so easy…

when I blame an appearance, am I not blaming You?
and when I overlook its limit, am I not lacking discernment…?

Oh Ease   Ease   Ease   Ease   Ease…   Ease…
would that I be neither more nor less of what 'me' is…

would that He, who encounters He when we are face to face,
countenance our reality…  even in our excess… presently…

27 October 2004

## Between Milan and Como

...so, I was looking at the bus driver
driving us from Milan to Como
speaking fluent Italian
- possibly even with a dialect -
his left hand on the wheel
and the right hand speaking Italian too
with that invisible woman
who sat at the front beside him,
the rain tapping vigorously
on the windscreen rubbed down
by the rhythmical swing of the wipers
to the right and the left,
while simultaneously the horizon
accelerating towards us
split itself continuously to
our right and the left

Nothing was really out of the ordinary
except for this melting sensation in my heart
when it knew that You are the
driver who speaks Italian so beautifully.
And it could see how all that was there
in the bus and outside it
going from Milan to Como
and accelerating towards us
from Como to Milan
was in motion.
Breathing or not,
all was in motion
always from You to You
without ever leaving.
I was not between Milan and Como
I was between You and You

7 November 2004

## Abraham

I met Abraham on Mount Moriah... after greeting each other in the name of the same all-presence present in his time and mine, we sat on the rock and I said to him... my

father I have come to trade my share given to you and your seed for everlasting eternity from Yahweh Elohim... tell Him, one of my daughters from the line of Isaac is

asking to trade her right over any land of dispute... tell Him, in return, let her into the land of the heart of Man... the land in which the only discrimination is Your

discernment between Your all-inclusion of Yourself and Your all-exclusive repudiation of anything other or equal to Yourself... and I said to him, my father, were I to be one

of your daughters from the line of Ishmael, even then tell Him, take the gifts You have granted me by the rocks for a sanctuary beyond the furthest limit... I said to

him, my father, I have come to trade my share with you... all the qualities bestowed upon me by the entirety of your seed with which you have determined your

nations, take back for His single identity... Abraham then stood up and I stood too... he wrapped my hands in his and moved them upwards from his chest to his lips and then

to his forehead... then he embraced me and said, my child, you have indeed chosen what was singled out for all mankind... before Adam was between water and mud

8 November 2004

## When Dead Before Death

...and at times, well before faiths dawn to worship
I whisper in my soul's ear, wake up!... wake up!...

will you not let He, who deems a martyr, martyr
when dead before death, reclaim your breath today...?

how else will you recognise Man... the Martyr...
in whom the Praised in all praised is Witness of Himself?

16 November 2004

## Sabbath

...when You make me stop
attributing existence to myself
altogether
I rest in You
and when You move me
with Your movement
I rest in You

I ask your Lord Oh Friday
not only on the sixth
I ask your Lord Oh Saturday
not only on the seventh
I ask your Lord Oh Sunday
not only on the first
but in every single day
and every single night
let me rest in You

17 November 2004

## Love for Certain

In the midst of terror
I have not separated
You from Yourself
by setting You up
into two camps
of Light and darkness
of Peace and war
or Good and evil

Because You are the one
named by all names;
the single indivisible identity
of all mankind
including that of the murdered
the murderer
and me

In the midst of terror
You are the real in all
and the mark
of the real in man is union
and union
is the wisdom of peace
and peace
is not that kind which
comes with a cease-fire
nor with the cosmo-polite.
In the midst of terror
Your peace is total
it includes war

In the midst of terror
You have separated
me from myself and held me
in Love for certain

26 November 2004

## I Never Cease

He whom you love
and who seemingly
ceased to be
never was
nor was he ever
going to be
any other
than Me
being him

So when you weep
for him whom you
will no longer see
I weep for you
for not seeing Me

26 November 2004

## As You Are

When I know
myself by myself
I neither know myself
nor anyone else

When I know
myself by You
You know Yourself
as me in and out

When I know
You by Yourself
You see Yourself
as You are

28 November 2004

## Who is Elect?

Oh
Adam

at this very instant
you are the utter mankind
reverberated in each human mystery

9 December 2004

## Why?

Words came one by one
and embraced grief

(...grief,
contorted in the grip
of asking why!?
but why!?...)

Moses is fresh...

*Hear Israel
the Ipseity, our God,
is One Ipseity*

Jesus is fresh...

*Life is to know Thee
that Thou art
God alone*

God to the Prophet is fresh...

*I was like a hidden treasure
and I loved to be known
so I created the Universes
that I might be known...
so that you know*

Oh Love-to-be-known
today even grief is shown
the reason we live
is also the cause of death

12 December 2004

## Hear Love's Hover

An object standing
in the way of
a very fast moving air
sounds like wind

A life standing in the
way of another fast
moving living,
may sound to some
like a fatal fate

I heard of a few who
hear but Love's Hover
Verbing Its Nouns anew

12 December 2004

## If

If you are bored with
conventional greeting
try the following

Jumble up ten words
from a greeting
card between brothers
and read it randomly

/ the / Ishma'el / Greatest /
/ Happiness / you / Dear /
/ wishing / Isaak / love / with /

...and you could try again

/ you / Isaak / love /
/ wishing / Dear / with / the /
/ Greatest / Ishma'el /
/ Happiness /...

...and again

/ Ishma'el / wishing / Greatest /
/ Dear / the / Happiness /
/ Isaak / love / with / you /

...and again
...and again
...and again...
...~~even if you~~,
even if by now we all knew

12 December 2004

## The Magnitude of Love

without you, Magnified, Love is sad.

where, otherwise, does the In Out?
where does the Above Below?
the First Last?
the Be Now?
the Image Mirror?
the Universe Manifest?
where does Language Verb?
where does the One Many?

without you, Magnified
where does the Before End
and the End More?
where does the Who How
and the How Do?
oh you, *if not for you*,
where does the Mine 'I'
and the 'I' Mine?

13 December 2004

## Day of Din

Are You using them
to test us or to punish?
Or to bring those You like
closer to You,
long before their Day of Din?

---

The Day of Judgment in Arabic - *Yawm I-Din*, in Hebrew - *Yom ha-Din*

15 December 2004

## The Breath of Kêdem

I caught a gleam
in that split second
before my glare turned flare...
as if I saw my own anger
like the hot winds of Kadîm
giving way to Kêdem
and its Breath of Rahamîm

How feeble is my tolerance
compared with Your Expanse
towards Your own Total Mass

---

Kêdem - in Hebrew, east, prior. A Divine Name for the most ancient origin.
Kadîm - in Hebrew, a scorching east wind, God's wrath.
Rahamîm - in Hebrew, Compassion. (Rahman in Arabic is the breath of the Compassionate Self).

15 December 2004

## Today

Today
the way to You
is already in You
from You
to You
with You
through You...
as it always was
yet today, this is as easy
as Your Ease is
when You are the means
Oh You to You
whose In
is without in
and From
is without from
and To
is without to
and With
is without with
and Through
is without through

17 December 2004

## Who Love Sees

Walking a bare heart outdoors
can so easily turn into abashment...
it is as if the Intimate
is magnified in the eyes...
strangers are attracted to You.
21st Century predators
mistakenly thinking it's me...
and me,
have I not seen strangers?
have I looked at Your Era
with eyes privy to Thee?

You startled me...
Oh Bewilderer,
if my trembling state
is Your call to conceal
what or who Love sees
please
don't hide it from me too
don't hide me from You

19 December 2004

## Demand Now

Your Names circling in the air
a demand rises in a chest
burning with desire
insisting silently
out of rhythm
be Evident now!
Evident now!
Now!
Now!

...and I could hear
simultaneously
my censor's reprimand:
What a lack of good form!
Who dares face the One
with demands?!

I didn't stop
even when You reminded him
If I am the Desirer
when I am the Desired
am I not the Demander
when I am the Demanded?

19 December 2004

## Breathe Compassion

If in Unity
not only
You are the Actor
in every action
but even the Acted-upon
why then
need I be offended?
Why need I be defended?

What did my first breath know
that this instant has forgotten?

Oh Breath
should I worry
about my fullest potential
if I breathe Compassion...
if my heart melts
liquid in my hand?

I raise my hands to the Victor,
too late to convert me
between X, Y or Z...

my heart is like a toddler
learning to speak...

who is now petrified?
who is now mercified?
who is the bewildered?

19 December 2004

## Certainty Waste

an image came...
the pacifiers of fears
say
the only certainty in life
is that we shall all die
and
after a pompous pause
they add
the only unknown is when...

what a pity...
what a certainty waste...
knowns and unknowns
could leave a chest
just like that...
be it ready or not...
and then what?
who will live deadcertain
of never leaving Ever's taste?

19 December 2004

## Damascus Market

If we
- like our early nomad fathers -
had left behind us
trails of stone mounds on our path
each time we encountered
the presence of the beloved
all the mountains would have been flattened by now
and all the valleys and all the oceans filled

One day perhaps
when the borders of the earth
open their gates to their chests
if you see me in the heart of Damascus market
I will not have pilgrimed a fraction from mine

19 December 2004

## Walk Away

ask it
what is your condition?

if it says any other than
only the Real has none
walk away
walk away

27 December 2004

## My Mother's Tongue

You might rightly say, brother
by my country of birth
it is modern Hebrew
and by my mother's country
it is Arabic, Qur'ánic
and by her ancestors
Babylonian Hebrew
the Aramaic of the Bible

Yet an ancient Name appeared
who nursed me from her Light
and she said
my mother is the most ancient
she speaks the existence of all

Light kills.
Light killed me with every suckle
and will reap many more deaths
even if my lips be weaned off
all mothers but Hers…

Now, she bursts
into thunderous laughter…
had you not been a rebel
- She giggles -
would your godless mother
need shout so often
*Indeed they belong to God and
most certainly to Him they return…?*

Salutations to all mothers
and to my midwife - Love
who sometimes disguises herself
amongst other things
as archaeo-modern English…

And after that, brother
would you mind much
which one you learnt
which one you forget
which is right
which incorrect
if Mother spoke you
even for one instant?

---

*Indeed… - Qur'anic - Inna lillah wa-inna ilayhi raji'un*

8 January 2005

## The Earth Answered

who would have thought
that out of all
the unlikely places abroad
the ground under one of my feet
would start talking... as Lover...
about Love... to me... in Switzerland...
and the ground
under my next step
follows in converse...
and Lago di Lugano...
and the dazzling white peaks of the Alps
crowning my head...
my Beloved is smiling...
nodding the head of a total stranger
greeting me 'bon journo' in passing

surely, Switzerland
you will forgive the folly amazement
of a heart exhausted with pleading?
but it was the Earth who answered:
if I were to draw upon my face
a random circle around your standpoint
and place your heart on its circumference
let's say
in Firenze
or Cannes
or Dijon
or Stuttgart
or Dachau
or Venezia...
should it make the slightest difference
where Love might speak?

delighted
I seized the moment of intimacy with Earth:
please tell my forefather,
the Babylonian Psalmist, tell Ibn Gabirol,
your right hand has not been forgotten.
ask them
is it because you did not forget Jerusalem?
ask them
if it was Love you remembered even more
would not Love
be remembered in your hand?

---

Solomon ben Yehuda ibn Gabirol. Lat. Avicebron (c.1022-c.1070). Poet and philosopher, one of the outstanding figures of Jewish "Golden Age" in Spain.

17 January 2005

## Against me for me

if You are the only Odd
who is the same as all the odds
who or what is there to stand against You?
who or what is there to stand against whom?

oddly, when all the odds standing against me
are from my very own disparate plurality,
You are the best Odd against me
who is entirely for me
whether I live
or die

18 January 2005

## Be Neither

My earth says, be still!
My heaven says, move!

But will I listen to Love when it tells
you can never become the becoming
so be neither still nor move

Beauty unveils herself
between the Beheld and the Beholder

19 January 2005

## I Wonder...

who could count time saying
there is but One Self?

Oh you, who hear a soundchest and not say to it
Oh no... no... you can't say One before you see...

Oh you, who counts two in-to-n-fro... so what?...
how many came to One without any seesaw?...

and I wonder... should I really mind who might mind
if I, too, say whosee who before One is in my eye...?

21 January 2005

## Come, Sit with me?

there is no remorse without it being already from the Mercifier
a gift bringing the far closer

Come, sit with me?

21 January 2005

## You are not my Lord

Herewith a strong wind
herewith a body
which, given a choice
would naturally incline
to seek refuge in God
in a mild
air-conditioned
Liberal Democracy

Herewith a strong wind
scaring the hell out of me.
Formal prayers are useless now
like the heap of down
hiding me under, top to toe

I said to the wind
by God
if I fear you
I make you my lord
and though
my Lord is all
- I agree -
you are neither my Lord
nor are you lording me!
And just like that
the wind let me be

One day
I shall invite
both the wind and my fear
to enter Peace in my heart

22 January 2005

## I Give Up

questions, questions, questions...
I give up...
what is my question?...
what would You have me ask You now?...
for Your utmost pleasure?...

23 January 2005

## Shocking

what could be more shocking
than the closeness of oneness?

so be shockliquate in bewilderment

Oh shock de-liberate
you are subscribed
with slaves
content

23 January 2005

## ||: Da Capo, Ad Infinitum :||

||: Whichever is my business
let me let it be Your Business
so that You be the Buyer
and You be the Maker
and You be the Seller
and You be the Buyer :||

...a heart
seized and twiddled in the presence of Love
was never converted...

23 January 2005

## Mercy, Mercy Speak

The scents of the Clement
have reached my breath...
I thought them sweet
soothing
but they ignite me
torch of remorse...

Oh...
how I dread my sight
in the mirror of fire!
Go apathy, go
and don't protest
but I am your defence
as the Mirror proclaims
apathy is so so callous!

I waive my rights by men
yet claim a remedy to mercify
a heart blind to Compassion

Mercy, Mercy
speak before me!
From its very first breath
my soul has forgotten
its Mother's Tongue.
Mine is high
proud above the dust
stupid, mean, stale, pretentious...
Mercy, Mercy
my tongue is defected
If you don't speak first
what point is there in my say
even if all will vouch kindly
'go ahead, talk, you are safe'?

The scents of the Clement
sweet and soothing
are now in my breath wonderment...
with what other than Mercy
could I approximate my gait
to Beauty's magnitude
as She approaches?

27 January 2005

## Get Message from this Era

I said to myself
I bid you abhorred restraint...
for once, let me Get Msg
from this era before Delete, lest
I deny my pains in my Far West

...so, today's supply and demand,
what do they indicate about my ailments?
that I can withstand the numbness of distance?
that I can't bear the throbbing of Closeness?

both?

28 January 2005

## I am a Missile

I am a missile launched
not from the point
where the death of the furthest west
gives birth to light
in the darkness of the furthest east
once every twentyfour hours

I am a missile launched
not from the Big Bang pictured today
by its own bedazzling incandescence
at the beginning of the Universes

I am a missile launched
not even from beyond the modern zodiac
where latest technology
might unravel the ethereal tomorrow

Had I not been homed in
onto the impact of Love
could I have known my launcher
who is otherwise the Hidden?

7 February 2005

## Empty Suitcase

I can hear the seasons say at this very instant
that at this very instant She travels weightless
in my empty suitcase...

Oh Solomon
here is good news under the Sun

18 February 2005

## Perhaps

Make a new covenant
with the whole of my body
so that perhaps my right hand
will stop saying
'God has chosen me'
'I am the first'
'I am the last'
'I am the best'
while it stabs my left

If I were God
- God forbid
and forgive the analogy -
how ridiculous would it be
for my hands to quarrel
each claiming it is me
to the exclusion of the other?

18 February 2005

## At Zero Greenwhich

Is there a party on either side
of the Prime Meridian
neither moved by the national
the religious
or the atheist aspect?

Neither moved by the right
the left nor the centre?
A party
not moved by a colour
nor a banner?
Is there a party
moved by Love's Perspective?

At Zero Greenwhich
under her Majesty's Dominion
will I be deemed traitor
or an utter fool for asking?

23 February 2005

## I, Israel, Ask

Will You call a heart
for Your betrothal
without giving it Hearing?
Will You then not give it the Vision
with which You behold Your Being?

Oh heart
see how even Pharaoh
is redeemed at once
between His lips
closing in on him
amidst the Red Sea reeds
as he professes
*You are the only Ipseity*.
Will you bear to be
incapacitated in oneness?
Mercified in nothingness?

I saw a big tree of ivy
with many branches;
each of a
different botanical species;
each afflicted
with a malady for its kind

The sword of the love of Truth
'shall I sever them all?'
The Mother of Nature, hesitant,
'cut!'
and I
- recognizing that that tree was me -
said 'go ahead, operate!'

You call me for my heart's betrothal
and I, Israel, ask, unveil Your bride

---

Bride - *Kalah* in Hebrew, from the root
*kol,* total, means also annihilated.

4 March 2005

## January is a Dog

no… January is more like the jaws of a dog-madly-in pursuit after its tail… chase, chase, chasebarking… chase… chaseresting… chasewaiting… chasesneaking…

chasebarking… barkingwhining… whining… whining… whiningfaintly… faintlystopping… stoppingforgetting… whiningforgetting… whiningforget… whiningforgot… forgot…

I must be careful what I say to January so as not to sound condescending… after all is there a thing I know January doesn't…? a new angle which might rekindle

January's spark…? what…? that any state of affairs is Love's affair…? that heads and tails are but a flip of one coin…? what…? that in Love there is not an 'inside'

outside-of-which Her embrace does not conceal…? or… that there is no farness distant by as much as a fraction from Her pulse…? from Her impulse…?

what is the matter with you?
Oh January, talk to me, what ails you…?

9 March 2005

## Gladden my Face

If I linger before you with torment
it is neither out of loneliness
nor to unload or find favour

but She engages
at this moment

per chance
you be a fresh breeze
from Her sweetness
to gladden my face

2 March 2005

## Nothing and No-one

I circumambulated my axis
at the heart of a cyclorama
of polished mirrors.
The last of them
precedes the first beside him
awaiting his turn at the end

I approached my image
in the mirror of Adam
and as soon as his pupil held mine
it said
*I am to my eye what Adam is to Him*
*so beware, beware*
*do not linger anywhere!*

I bowed my head
my right hand on my chest
and continued thus with each
till I saw my image in the mirror of Job.
My image
pulling my hands to my face
like calyx under a corolla
pleaded:
*Stop here, you have reached your goal.*
*Can't you see your distinctions in him?*
I smiled with great affection at my face
in the mirror of Job, and said
*Yes. I do. Bless you, bless you*
*but I am warned to go on*

I proceeded bowing one by one
till I faced my image
in the mirror of the last
asking me
*What do you see?*
  *Me.*
Motioning me to come closer
he asked
*Now what do you see?*
   *My details clearly,*
  *some fair some ugly.*
Then, at utmost magnification
*What do you see?*
  *Nothing.*
*Who do you see?*
  *No-one.*
At that point Intimacy said
*I have conquered them all*

6 May 2005 Chisholme House

## I Do!

on the day of the green I asked my tears, what prompted you?
am I pitying myself? am I yearning for Him or praising His Mercy to me?

who is crying anyway if *He is and there is not with Him a thing?*
They said do, do go out, wash in the dew, and I am dewface, dewgaze

ingathering  sparkle  scatter  widewet  carpetever  coolgreen  sparklewho
who beckoned? me! me! I am the only... who beaconed me? no! no! I am He!

Go! go ifonly... go onlyif... who could know Only inOnly  ininfinite  indiverse
inscattersyntax  inLeading  inmisleading  inawayfrom  intowards?

Today I shall become established in the happiness and love of weepingin
hearingof sightof touchof gaitof tasteLoveitself itself claims its due:

I do! I do! I do! I do!...  Oh four corners, will you be witnesswielded?
if today there is but one 'I Do', who weeps for who?

18 May 2005

## Kisses upon Kisses

would that we knew... this instant... the timeless...
would that Beauty stripped herself naked, her love making

is speech in one ear and music in the other...
no cacophony is ruled out of her muse... in kissing

kisses upon kisses, one and one, and, one by one,
and, billions upon billions... here, she is kissing herself

into being, and here, she is kissing herself out of being...
perhaps a little break for her relativity's exhaustion...

would that we knew this instant the timeless, are we the
walkers walking in her love affair of infinity infinitizing?

Oh, how we love our era, or, should one say,
Oh, how our era loves itself now...

and you, what do you see?
would that Beauty dropped off a few of her layers for you,

could you see her kissing herself into your pains of distance,
into your pleasures of closeness... all at once?

28 May 2005 Chisholme House

## Love is Didactic

I said to my friend

People will shout at me
For being didactic,
But this is how it is;
Love is Didactic -
It loves to be known.

He wrote it down and said
here, you've got another one

12 June 2005 M6 to Oxford

## A Sad Fashion Designer

Look at me!
Have you seen a mammoth
showered with so many thousands of praises
who, whilst the eyes of those he dressed
- riveted to their new image in the mirror -
turned more and more joyous;
his, however
have turned so so sad, lamented?

Where is my Mirror?
Will I, unlike them,
find it by undressing myself naked?

Oh, how this mammoth bull aches
for the proximity of the china.
Look at me! A big mammoth crying:
where is my place?

Is it in the sweetness of my aching
for the Subtle's subtling?
for the Gentle's gentling?

15 June 2005

## A Concrete Noun in Hell

I called Her names
all of them
and spoke with urgency
I suffer with your sickness!
You are abstract nouns;
intangible states in constriction.
I am a concrete noun in hell!

One moment
I brim remorse
I need your utter clemence
- lest it was I who prevented
your collective verbation -

and another
I am fury!
Forget your eminent ranks
I shout
can a contingent decree any effect!?
can I? can you? can we?

Yet another
I am attention,
what if I miss Her in my deafening blare
should She come running...
should She be here...presently

Gushing amidst states and potencies
Love plucks heart after heart
from the epicentre of instant after instant
and drops them
right into the joyous isthmus of dispassion...
now they rest...reset...
She is Instant...Omnipresent

Oh She who is He
who is we who is me,
mine is not with Thine
but with Thee

24 June 2005

## How Strange...

how strange is Love!
she moves you backwards... towards your pre-existence

towards the torment of her qualities
who ache for their overflowing as you

how strange that the movement of Love should paralyse
you in expansion and expand you in contraction

how strange that this backward movement towards
your original pains is in fact a leaping progress forwards

how so incomparably so irrevocably attractive!
how strange is Love...

your pains... have they turned yet pangs of longing?
they're hers, love... polishing you to see herself best

2 July 2005

## The United Nations

By what?
By their nationality?
Or by the one being of their humanity?

I saw the house in a new dress.
Surrounding it
its flags turned banners.
Their fabric
swallowed its symbols and colours
and manifested the names
of Man in their stead.

Thus, at once,
the banners stood collectively
for each and all the nations
as well as every single heart
in their diverse human palette.

And I, a Babylonian Israelite,
what have I seen?
Have I seen
the end of the beginning?
the beginning of the end?
the end without end?
Have I seen the heart of Zion
with the 'I' of Being?
Have I seen my heart?

22 July 2005

## ...and before that...

...last night a giant orange full moon is racing my left side suddenly i know the road is turning... it is facing us now straight ahead... perplexity

perplexity... your signs, what do they say upon my horizon?... and before that i apologise to a waiter for complaining... he is pleased and pacified even

before i tell him why... and before that we pick and eat ripe cherries from tree after tree while walking back towards the car and before

that strolling in a narrow foot path amidst a golden field of wheat... like the one i pictured closed eyed with a flemish farmer cropping it with

a scythe and before that a woman is buying an outfit in the sale a blue saphire jacket made of double crepe silk moroccain £144 a kingfisher silk

crepe de chine top... i look at her eyes... £96 a kingfisher silk Matka skirt £60 a french silk chiffon scarf with blues turquoise and aqua marines

merging smoothly one with the other £120 and another silk moroccain skirt but in a bright aquamarine £96 totaling £576... and before that

trying them on not even a shred of a need to persuade her to stick to one colour or fabric arises because it all looks good exciting

harmonious... and before that i continue to type a letter and before that a woman is buying an outfit and before that I beg her firmly to try on

the matching skirt as well she does and they rejoice before the mirror as if already in their daughter's wedding... and before that typing

a personal letter which though will be sent to hundreds it is You i address... and before that waking up in the middle of a dream ordinary

people are talking about You i say to them quite astonished how well you perceive unity utterly concordant with the divine order... oh perplexity

now is the dawn of last night's tomorrow... before long my horizon be filled with new surprises from before there was a before... prior to any prosperity

24 July 2005

## In the Middle

In the Beginning - Love
in the End - Love
even in the Middle - Love

And they
who quote Love from books
might say - concerning the middle -
that such a proposition is a denial of evil

And I
- between the causes and effects of living and dying -
if I have ever known Love by the Lover
I must have refrained from attributing Life to another

31 July 2005

## My Starting Point

Between You and me
You are the First
and I am Your last
but my starting point as Your last
does not begin with me
and though it requires my end
it neither ends me
nor does it end without me

So what is the end of me to me
if without me I remain eternally
with none but the Starting of all points?

31 July 2005

## A Paramoral Poet

When I look for the objective reporter of the instant
I look for the Eye of the One 'I' of the eyes of existence

A broadcast of news about passion - for instance - is at once
about the 'I' of fire and the 'I' of movement and the 'I' of life

and the 'I' of love and the 'I' of bewilderment and the 'I' of error
and the 'I' of terror and the 'I' of horror and the 'I' of

acceleration-into-stopping-at-once-in-the-middle-of-a-state...
and the 'I' of delight and the 'I' of light and the 'I' of the other light

and you, you go ahead now, you name it... who will then ask a
paramoral poet how can Love go with terror, or error with sight?

11 September 2005 M25 to Oxford

## Dare We?

nothing stands between your heart and mine
except your you and my me...

dare you move from yours a mortal fraction?
dare I move from mine?

dare we see Love in Love with Love
in every kind of relation?

dare we verify...?
dare we testify?
dare we...?
darewe?

21 September 2005

## Jump in Dirty

Oh miserable gloomy soul
- so I talk with myself -
why postpone yourself from this instant
saying
when I shall be purified I'll be in union, then...
...or, after all I'm only a student now...
...or, I'm only in preparation, not yet ready...
...as if the preparation towards union
is not already from union in union...

...who is the student, I wonder,
who can study a thing about unity
if not learnt with the act of the uniter
in that which
was
is
and forever will be
united?

Will the air say
hang on a minute
I shan't be inhaled unless you're pure?

Oh miserable chaser of horizons
come
jump into this instant
dirty

21 September 2005

## Verb the Cow into Union

Words are all nouns
and
nouns are already verbations
of
the one named by all
from
the most superlative to gobbledygook
so much so
that
I have to remind myself
- every-now-and-then -
say
when I drink milk
that
it might be the complete verbation of 'cow'
if
I become the verbation of 'me'
by
absorbing her milk not only into my bloodstream
- and consequently into my thoughtstream -
but
right up - or down - into the reverberation
of
Union

23 September 2005

## Lord of Dictionaries

                      ...and grammar of inspiration
and of human right
              to be the meaning of Man
and of equality
     wherein closeness
                is by singleness of origin
and of opportunity
            to be grabbed by Your best
and of freedom of speech
              in silence of the partial
and the right to remain silent
             while truth is speaking
and of law of return
            from anger to compassion
and of fifth amendment
     as if there is anywhere
        in Your constitution
           where I could hide from myself
Oh Lord of dictionaries
            and inspiration of grammar
    just save me
      save me therein
     from the
          supposititious

4 October 2005

## In Combustion

Israel, is not what Israel
thinks Israel is...
...because Israel
in Oneness,
doesn't exist
other than
the verb Man

See these secular hands?
These secular hands have never lit a Shabat candle.
Could hands or candles ignite a heart?

See this chest in combustion?
In combustion
that which Speaks
says
I am the Jew
the Capulet the Montague
the Mary the Elizabeth the blood between
I am the eyes lacrimating on the frail Dame Cecily's hands
the dagger sparing Isaac's jugular on the Moriah
the green and pleasant pastures of Yir'êh'hu-Shalêm
the sacred arrow of the plains
brushing by the hair without killing
the beauty scars on the face of Abêr
the carved stone of Yanus
the whale swallowing Yunus
the Sunni the Shi'ite the milk of their camel
the Psalmist weeping for Zion
in the confluence of the waters of Babel
I am Chün tzu and the sound of one hand clapping
I am the Pictograph
the Cuneiform
the Rune
I am the Aleph-Beth of United Kingdom

Salim, is not what Salim
thinks Salim is...
...because in Taslim
Man is the verb Him

10 October 2005

## How are You?

Oh instant, Oh breath, Oh place,
Oh Love-to-be-known, how are you?
what good news have you from He, who is
unknowable, to me, who is none other than Him?

they said at the open portal, when you enter the Heart of Man
place upon the altar of He who is unknowable
the whole of existence
in-question

18 October 2005

## Drown in Pleasure

If there is only the One
and nothing but,
who might you be?
who might I?
who might we?

Come
come drown in the pleasure of a gathering
the pleasure which turns increasingly sweet
when a spontaneous silence descends upon it

21 October 2005

### *Hinêh ma Tov*  Sitting in the Singular

| | |
|---|---|
| *Hinêh mah tov* | Look here how so beneficent |
| *'umâh na'îm* | and how so pleasant |
| *shêvet akhîm gam yâkhad* | is the sitting of those, not other in the Singular |

---

Psalm 133; 1, rendition from Hebrew

21 October 2005

## My Soul    *Nafshî*

Neither my heart outranked Your height    *Lo gavâh libî*
nor my eyes surpassed Your sight    *velo ramû 'eynây*
nor have I usurped Your marvels and might    *velo hilâkhti bi-gdolôt uvenifla'ôt mimêni*

Have I not faced You and silenced my soul    *Im lo shivîti ve-domâmti nafshî*
like one weaned off his ma?    *cagamûl 'alêy imô*
So is my soul weaned off me    *cagamûl 'alây nafshî*

---

Psalm 131 rendition

29 October 2005

## Have I imagined?

I must have imagined
I opened an account
here on earth
without any deposit

That I, made of clay,
withdrew my priority today
- the intangible Image of Man -
out from its sphere in heaven
then, impressed it upon
one of the moods of fire in my chest
till it dwindled in its capital - nought!

Perhaps I have imagined
I opened an account
from which, the more I drew
the more I grew accustomed
in my Capital - inexhaustibly rich already

22 November 2005

## What is the Taste of Union?

My goodness!
This is not about asking
to be moved
from pessimism to optimism.
Not even from despair to hope.
Oh no!
They're all useless traits
of the partially blind

This is about the taste
of stamping my foot
in my chest
and lo and behold
all fade out but the 'I' who
could uninterruptedly say
I am the Only
in each and every sense or state

23 November 2005

## Copy Rights

Yes…do help yourself lest
without my consent we both end up thieves:
you from me, and I, from the eye in my chest

So help yourself if must albeit you already have it
and in your chest's eye
it is best

25 November 2005

## Woe to a Lover

Woe to a lover
who knows not
his real Beloved is many

Today
*thy enemy*
and
*thy neighbour*
are
*as thyself*
none other than the One
who Loves His own self as you, as we

\*\*\*

They say every bullet has a name... Oh index, how many a foe
would you strike off the list today if you knew there is but One Named?
and if not moved by Love's impact, what else could remove you from the trigger
so as to move a mountain with a pen, or better still,
point by the Index of all?

28 November 2005

### ...So Corollarate

So basically
that the corolla is its petals,
that, we all agree

but
if the One is not
you
and me
and he
and she
and they
and them
and it
and we
and We
then
what is the One's corollary?

Does not any contrary
- Heaven forfend -
mean that you or me
are the Divine Crown,
the Absolute Deity?

7 December 2005

## Detachment Woke me

Detachment woke me
in the silence before dawn
demanding contemplation

7 December 2005

## They Laughed

and said
don't be fooled by our beginnings
we are all from a single instant
in the Timeless

11 December 2005

One Lip    *Safâ Ahât*

...the earth globally is one lip with a few words    *...kol-ha'ârets safâ ahât u-dvarîm ahadîm.*

...there is but one nation and one lip to all    *...'am ehâd ve-safâ ahât le-khulâm*

---

Genesis 11; 1, 6, rendition from Hebrew
Lip - *safâ* - language

11 December 2005

## What is Said is Seen    *Ashêr Ye'amêr Yera'êh*

And Abraham called / *Vayikrâ Avrahâm*
the name of that place / *shem hamakôm hahû*
He Sees / *Yehovâ yir'êh*
for that which is said / *ashêr ye'amêr*
today upon His mount / *hayôm behâr Yehovâ*
is made evident / *yera'êh*

---

Genesis 22; 14, rendition from Hebrew

Abraham renamed *'Ir Shalêm* (whole city) *Yehovah-yir'êh* (Yehovah sees), later it was changed to *Yir'ehu-shalem* (He saw it whole), then to *Yeru-shalêm* and finally to *Yerushalâyyim* (Jerusalem).

11 December 2005

## To Palestine from Israel

(...for are not the States of Nations like the states of a person who has forgotten he is one?)

\*\*\*

Oh Instant, Oh Breath, embrace all that which is in our past, present and future tense, as we are embraced in the Timeless before we determined upon time with our existence...

tell them, Adam, tell them *you* are coexistence,
tell them *you* are us without our limits...
tell Saul, tell her who sneers and sneers at dreams;

today, I am not the dreamer who believes in mankind...
nor am I the dreamer speaking... today, *you* are the narrator
of Amen... Amen... Amen...

---

Saul - Sha'ul Tchernichowsky b. Russia (1873-1934). Leading poet in early modern Hebrew. *Sneer, Sneer at Dreams*, is among his most well known sung poems:

"Sneer, sneer at dreams
'Tis I, the dreamer speaking
Sneer, for I do believe in Man
For I still believe in you"

17 December 2005

## What Say You?

What say you
Oh chest in waiting?
What say you
then,
when he who says
'You'
to He who says Be
to a word
and it is so becoming?

18 December 05

## A Word with You

Would that I be
my word with You
before, and without which
I am not I
and after which
I am not my I

18 December 2005

## Covering up the Apparent

How many times
have I demanded
transparency from another
without it instantly covering up
the Apparent?

24 December 2005

## Charged with Itself

The charge of the Dearest
is naught if not
charged with Itself

25 December 2005

## From which Essence?

When the Water waters
when the Earth earths
when the Fire fires
when the Air airs
from which essence
oh Nardin
sprays your descent?

---

Nardin - Nard or Spikenard in Persian, perfume native
of the Himalaya and highly prized in biblical times

26 December 2005 Chisholme House

## Give me to that Taste

Pains have long
shed their causes;
give me to that taste
in between Nearness
and yearning for closer

I have no head...
things are not things...
bodies are not bodies...
here all is stark naked;
the day is stark naked;
see? Stars cast no shade...

Give me to that taste
between In and More
wherein Light prior
to Light before light
is arrested in the continuum
of Darkness without darkness
without a pair
without a partner
without compare...

1 January 2006 Chisholme House

## An Adam Spat

Îmma Adamâ is Mother Earth;
She becomes rather like the Sun
spitting Herself all over Herself;
some mud and blood
and here I am,
an Adam spat in migration
or perhaps a view spat
from one point to another aspect
only to-be-held apogee
by a global Dimension...

...then...
what distance or difference
might there be between
your mud and mine
if Mother Herself is
the high
and low
and far
and near
and this and that
and here and there
and all that which is in between?

1 January 2006 Chisholme House

## Ha Ha! She'd Better!

December and January
are kissing and faking a treaty
about direction and intention
and what is backward
and what ahead
and pretend they sincerely
care about me

December worried possessively;
is she really lost to the transient?
January ready to mock, cynical...
Ha ha! She'd better! How else
is she to face the Most Ancient?

## To Nogah

לנוגה

and what will the Bright irradiate
were he not touched and drawn
since before the Origin shone?

ומה יניה הנוגה
אם לא נוגע ונהה
מקידמת נהרת האורה?

will she, the gloomy, glow
unless awoken illuminate?

התניה הנוגה
בלתי אם ניעורה נאורה?

Here is a deep breath and here is a long blow
over birthday candles flickering in a Georgian house
under a capricious Scottish sky crying drizzles of
solidarity (of happiness...? of sadness...?
for the distant unknown...? who knows...?)

הנה נשימה עמוקה והנה נשיפה ארוכה
על נרות יום הולדת מהבהבים בבית ג'ורג'יאני
תחת כיפת שמים סקוטיים קפריזיים בוכים
זרזיפי סולידריות (של שמחה....? של עצב...?
על רוחק הבלתי ידוע...? מי יודע...?)

I wonder who is the new drop to remember itself
an ocean in the cloud and a cloud in the ocean
while still wondering in the kingdoms of the land?

תוהני מי הטיפה החדשה שתזכור עצמה
אוקיאנוס בענן וענן באוקיאנוס
כאשר עדיין נעה ונדה במלכויות היבשה?

---

Written in Hebrew and rendered into English

## Unquenchable

## בלתי ניתן לרוויה

Oh He who is Omnipresent with all in His All
Oh He with whom there is not one living soul
if a slight echo or a murmur were to sound
it is He, His Spirit's hover, humming

and though I, between He and He,
am but a middle by His immediacy
thirst for Him shall never die nor quench
for it is no longer mine
but His own thirst for Himself

הו הוא ההוה כולו עם כולו בכולו
הו הוא אשר אין עמו נפש אחת חיה זולתו
לו נשמעה בתקול קלילה או אוושה חלשה
רחיפת רוחו היא היא אשר הומה

ואף שאני ביני לבינו
אינני אלא אמצע באמצעותו
לעולם לא יכלה ולא ירווה צמאון אליו
כי אינו עוד צמאוני שלי
אלא צמאונו שלו אל עצמו

---

Written in Hebrew and rendered into English

8 January 2006 Chisholme House

| | |
|---|---|
| **בהמיית הוא** | In the Hum Hu |
| מעולם לא באתי | Never have I come |
| ולא התישבתי | or settled down |
| אלא אם היתה | unless it was |
| המיית המילה הוא | the hum of the Word Hu |
| שהוציאתני הנה | which brought me hither |
| ולא הטיפה הסרוחה | and not the putrid drop |
| | |
| ולא אל רימה ותולעה אשובה | and I return not to maggot and worm |
| ולא תצא נפשי | nor shall my soul expire |
| לא אל עפר הארץ | to the dust of the earth |
| ולא אל מרומי על | or the heights above |
| אלא אל | but towards |
| המיית הוא | the hum Hu |
| בהמיית הוא | in the hum Hu |

---

Written in Hebrew and rendered into English
Hu - the absolute pronoun He in the semitic languages

11 January 2006 Chisholme House

## The Grounds of Being

When in Rome
be like the Man
who rendered all existence to God
thereby honouring the Roman
well beyond his utmost praise
or Caesar's dearest prize

11 January 2006 Chisholme House

## Look who's Speaking

If it is what it is
then what it is is speaking
and you and me... what speaks us?

aargh 'you'... aargh 'me'
how might it be we, if we are not we?
if there is not aught but He?

11 January 2006 Chisholme House

## Jerusalem

No time elapsed in the Presence since our last encounter
and even before my question had set Abraham hastened;

this was said today on His mount; *there is but One Self*
and this was made evident; *only the Self Sees the Self*

At that moment all that has ever been severed
was peaced-upon with He who Re-membered

12 January 2006 Chisholme House

## Where Love Loves Love

*Oh ye daughters of Jerusalem*
wide awake is Love
where the hearts are melted
and the eyes arrested

Oh you who asks
who is my beloved?
Oh you who asks
who is my lover?
Oh you who asks
who loves when I love?
Oh you who asks
who is loved when I am loved?

Oh beauties awoken
were Love to love Love
where Love Loves Love
have a rest too, do have a rest

5 February 2006

## An 'I' Inside Out

Here, one step
is a sudden airborn 'I'
no taking off
no soaring
no hovering
no landing
no falling

unshackled amid gravities
the Highest of all height
is Deepest of all depths
Darkness is Light
Darkness is Sight inside out

Here, 'I', is a step
not from this nor from that
thank goodness
I am not towards this
nor am I towards that
here is an 'I' inside out

5 February 2006

## The hhhh of He

Without the hhhh of He
from the innermost recesses
will the mid aaaaah of 'I'
utter the alphabets
into existence?

Without the hhhh of He
whose breath will recommence?

11 February 2006

## Your Hands Love

Now is all good
and all good is now...
give me your hands love
give me your hands

In the Ark of Triplets
those which are, are now
are to multiply
and those from before
and those from after
die indeed they die;

yea assents yea
noes to ayes
are noes denied
are noes delayed
let them then
let them be slayed

Your hands love
look at your hands.
See? all well is done
and all best arranged

19 June 2006

## In the 'I' of 'We'

Are you and me of those, who
still separate when they say 'I am'?
or of those who posh-up
their distinction with 'one is'?
or of those who
rank-it-up-or-down with 'we are'
while leaving some other 'we's out?

Are you and me of those, who
when they say we
they mean
Oh you, and you, and you,
this is how it is;
'I', plus 'I', plus 'I', don't add up to 'we'
yet 'I' is all 'we', and 'we' is all 'I'
without any addition or subtraction

So then, when we gather,
Oh desolate you and me,
in the 'I' of 'we' is the Cordial

25 June 2006

I
am
not
a
Racist

dearest
dearest
Blacks
and Reds
and Browns
and Yellows
and Green-Blue
eyed Whites
our instant
optical illumination
is in the
rays or Eye
of the
Colourless

and don't you dare
say
Oh Purples
and Oranges
that I am a racist
lest Mankind obliges
and you be granted a human face

25 June 2006

## Blind

When I orbit You, You orbit my eye...
then... this eye is not mine...
then... in Your Eye
all eyes are
blind

27 June 2006

## NeitherNor

in
how
many
breaths
Oh Happy
are You born
thus far?
out of
all the names
Adam chose
for existence,
which one
might he
choose
for
himself?
how many
instants
Oh Happy
does it take
to distance
You now
from my breath?
what
are names
to me
if NeitherNor
is the Heart where
names are
theirs
no more?
but You remain,
Oh Happy,
my heart
celeb
roam
run
roar
for storms
thunder
ahead
and
in their eye
I am
un-narrated
and in mine
not in the least
rare

29 June 2006

## How I-am-I Do

A heart can be talking with Love
like a finger is talking with its hand...

if I ask, how are You?
inquired the heart,
would You not say, I am I?

Love said, yea, I am I

so should I ask, how is it that
You-are-You, the Biggest,
is You-are-You, the most minute?

Love said
if you look from where
you-are-not-you,
here is how, I-am-I, the Whole,
is I-am-I, the part

so should I ask,
how You-are-You, the One,
do You-are-You, the many?
or just, how do You do?

ha... and how do you do?

now,
I-am-not-I,
is I-am-We-without-we;
and now,
We, is I-am-I without We

Yes, said Love,
this is how I-am-I do

30 June 2006

## Face to Face

              today     today
      I establish You     You establish You
      Lord upon lords     Face to Face
of 'I's and 'thou's and 'it's     I and Thou and It

2 July 2006

## Between All and None

...and if you ask me
what are you then?
are you a Kabbalist?
a Zen Buddhist?
a Christian?
a Shaman?
perhaps a Sufi?

...then
I'm obliged to say
that if you know the heart
to be the verb, Man
you'll already know
from your very own self
that what you are
is between all and none
thus what you are
and what I am
is utterly the same
in being and not being

...and if you don't know
or won't at least try
you might as well guess

2 July 2006

## Patience

did you sit with me

when I complained...?

I said to Patience

what a mystery...

of all Her agents

are you the slowest

and furthest away...?

are you the fastest?

the closest?

and my complaints...?

what of my complaints

if where you are

that which is in progress

is proxy for the most perfect

and the most perfect

is already with Beauty...?

2 July 2006

## Oh Lovechest

it is Love
who celebrates her timeless origin not only in your anniversaries
but at each moment in time between your birth and death...

but alas, Oh lovechest, would you care
to join her party presently
lest your next breath
is your
last?

4 July 2006

## When?

I said to myshe
Oh niggard eloquence
how will your race to Union succeed
if it's out of bounds of the game of the Victor
whose trophies are at once for you
each single instance you're speechless...?

4 July 2006

## Translate an Eve into Eye

who is saying all praise be to
One
bringinginto Union withwhen
you praise
He
praises
He
when you give
He
Gives
He
Receives
when you know yourselfin
He
Knows
all are inUnion
even those who may never see that when
they falloutoflove
Love
was already their w i n g e d L o v e r
their w i n g e d B e l o v e d . . . ?



Oh Twiddler-of-hearts between kernels and carnals a-mazed...
will You interpret cool-airs to the waters-blazed...?

when I was seized in Adam's pupil, when-dipped-down-into-being-
circumambulated-by-his-ribcage, Adam was-neither-a-man-nor-a-woman...

I asked her in the Parthenon of the selfadoring, oh my-she,
has anyone ever met gods or goddesses in Eden...?



Oh Interpreter of ardent desires... who would dare (metaphysically) save
an ardordazed dented under a man's palms inflaming...?

who'd dare tell her, burning in Eden leaves no odoursmoke no scar-ache
no cinders...? who asked me, did you really imagine Love a poem outside

your body...?   I say...   Oh You...   You translate an Eve into Eye...
You are me, and I... I am ever free between Your whys and Your Why...

4 July 2006

## Amidst Her Spires

Between the Works and the East Gate of the Ford of the Oxen, Oh Breath, upon whom shall I blow from the breeze of the Garden of Universaldiversity

if inbetween there is only room for one *I am...? I am,* be pleased to hailinto you from Rose Lane... Oh you... to be found in Love amidst Her Spires...

4 July 2006

Re-collection

what is new?
your heart as it re-collects
One, is all ways always glad tidings

4 July 2006

## Your Site of Encounter

I did not ask her, Oh Salma bint al 'Arabîyyah
who sent you to me, bint al 'Ibrîyyah?
instead, I said here, take this new black raiment
embroidered with the reds of your tribe
to remind you of its ancient elders... the Words...

and no more was mentioned of the splendour
and marvels of their dressing and undressing a metaphor...
or how they transpose food and drink from Time to time
or un-tether and chide their camel into motion
from the H of He through the A of Adam...

...and who am I to question Love's timing or measure?
Oh Love,
was not I, myself,
always the very brink upon which I lose sight?
...and who will,
even in my crave to love and be loved by the lesser,
magnify 'me' to 'us' right into Your Site of Encounter?

5 July 2006

## Lovethunderbolt

Oh Lovethunderbolt
all is mortal and immortal
and when You strike
Immortal

26 July 2006

## Interpreter of Twilights

Oh Joseph
Oh Lovechest in waiting

  do birds breakfast before
        singing at dawn?

have I drunk all my days at nights
...and will I gown all tomorrows' casts
        with a deep sleep sight?

      Her cool breeze does not skip
          a single window
              open
         to re-dreaming
         your life
        from Love
          upon
       Light
       upon
     Oh Height
  ...Oh Interpreter
    of twilights
   in the Isle
of Beaute

26 July 2006

## Her Musks at Dusk

Every time, Oh Time,
you strip me off myself, I strip you of yours
whereupon instantly Her Instant swallows us both
with all our added on reminders and protections

Her musks are free from prefix or suffix at dusk
when they standunder Her termination

Oh He, who says Be
to he who says He
from He to He
and he be
He

6 March 2007 a week in seclusion

## Talking to Love

don't see me that I'm talking to you,
I'm talking to Love...
and when I'm talking to Love
Love is talking to Love
and when Love is talking to Love
Love is hearing...
Love is hearing very well indeed...

## Towards Encompassing

From the earliest humanity, innovations were brought about in response to necessity in the best of arrangements, in adoration, in praise and the love of beauty. This response demonstrates the preponderance of our perfectibility well beyond our instinct to preserve our achievements. Human perfectibility is not only like a vault for what has been established superlatively, but it is the only 'universal organ' in which beauty's love to be known may unravel entirely, perfectly and in ever increasing new modes of expression.

It is in our perfectibility that what has to be, is shown together with its means whether its significance is fully apparent or not. For example, our ancient civilizations' writing systems have evolved in the Middle Bronze Age to their pinnacle synthesis, the Alphabet, providing for the first time one sign to represent a single sound of speech. (All alphabets today have been adopted and adapted from this first 22 letter Phoenician Aleph-beth, transmitted to the west through Greek and to the east by Aramaic.) One cannot but amaze at how this monumental contribution to humanity, hardly used by its inventors, appeared concurrently for the emergence and globalization of monotheism, coinciding with the entire eclipse of the ancient civilizations.

Either willingly or willy nilly, this order of evolution is inevitable. Yet there is no further spiritual progress other than that which begins without intermediary. And here we are, in the Early Silicon Age of the World Wide Web necessitated above all for its most prevalent of merits in the service of a new current of self awareness: direct immediacy. We are inevitably stepping into a new spiritual impulse towards encompassment *in* oneness. An impulse ultimately branding in humanity's heart the constitution for a Universal Vernacular.

**In the service of this emergence
our greatest privilege is the acknowledgement
that there is but One Indivisible Self
other than whom there is none**